Douglas Supon

How To Stay Positive in A Negative World

Awaken Your Inner Light and Rise Above the Darkness

The Guide to Living a More Positive Life

How to Stay Positive in a Negative World
© 2025 Douglas Supon

All rights reserved. No part of this publication may be reproduced, distributed, or transmitted in any form or by any means, including photocopying, recording, or other electronic or mechanical methods, without the prior written permission of the publisher, except in the case of brief quotations used in reviews or scholarly works.

ISBN: 9798285531500
Printed in United States
Independently published

Cover design by Douglas Supon
Edited by Mikayla Supon

This book is a work of nonfiction. While every effort has been made to ensure accuracy, the author makes no guarantees and is not liable for any outcomes resulting from the use of the information in this book.

You're Here—And That Means Something

Before you dive into this book, take a moment, and breathe.

The fact that you picked this up means you're looking for something—peace, hope, clarity, or maybe just a little encouragement. Whatever it is, I'm glad you're here.

You're not alone.

Life gets heavy. Minds get tired. Hearts feel overwhelmed.

But here's the truth: you have the power to shift your mindset, to protect your peace, and to build a better day—starting right now.

This book won't fix everything. But it will give you tools to help you stay grounded, find light in dark moments, and choose positivity even when it's hard.

You don't have to be perfect.

You don't have to have it all figured out.

You just have to start. Let's take this one step at a time—together.

Why I Wrote This Book

I wrote this book to reach out to others to help make a positive impact. The world can feel like a heavy place sometimes. Between the chaos on the news, the pressure of daily life, and the quiet battles we all face behind closed doors, it's easy to feel overwhelmed, discouraged, or even lost. I know what that feels like—not just from watching others, but from living it myself.

I believe, with every part of me, that positivity is not just a personality trait—it's a practice. It's something we can all build, even in the hardest moments. It doesn't mean pretending everything is perfect. It means choosing to look for hope, meaning, and strength even when things get tough.

This book is my way of giving back. It's for anyone who's ever struggled to keep going, felt stuck in a dark place, or needed a reminder that better days are possible. It's full of real, practical tools that helped me, and that I believe can help you too.

You're not alone. And staying positive isn't about ignoring the negative—it's about learning how to rise above it.

Let's do that together.

This is the first step to leading a more positive life. I decided to write this book to do my best to help others become more positive. Life can be incredibly hard, and we all face our own unique challenges. No one is guaranteed anything in life—not a single person. We all experience days and chapters that feel impossible. The world often seems overwhelmingly negative and difficult.

The good news is that this isn't true. The title of this book is How to Be Positive in a Negative World. But the thing is—it isn't really a negative world.

That's just perspective. The world actually has far more good in it than bad. Unfortunately, the ugly is what we tend to focus on or see.

Why is this? Well, negativity and drama sell. The news and social media mostly push out negativity and heartache. This is everywhere we look—news, social media, TV—and because of this, it's easier to see the negative side of the world we live in. This constant exposure can be draining for all of us.

Positivity is all around; you just have to work a little harder to find the good instead of the bad.

We all have this one amazing life to live, and we each face different struggles every day. I am going to show you how to find the good in the bad, and how to stay more positive in a negative world.

By the end of this book, I hope you'll have at least one good trick to help make your life more positive. There's a saying: we all live once and die once. But the truth is, we live every day. And we're all in this together.

STOP SAYING I CAN'T OR I WILL TRY

STOP SAYING "I CAN'T" OR "I WILL TRY":

Saying "I can't" or "I will try" already sets the mindset for failure. When we say it out loud or even to ourselves, we're giving our brains an easy way out. Planting that seed is like saying, "It's okay to fail" or "I will fail."

Failing is okay if you learn from it— but it's always better to approach something by saying, "I will" or "I can." Speaking positively feeds your mind and strengthens your drive for success.

This is all about mindset. And the right mindset helps prepare you to complete the task ahead.

You can and will do it.

Smile More

Smile More:

This might sound a little silly at first. Some may wonder, "How can smiling more really make me feel better or more positive?" But the truth is, smiling—though it takes a little effort—has a powerful effect.

It's actually easier not to smile. Smiling uses between 5 and 53 facial muscles, and it requires a conscious decision. But that small choice to smile can change your whole mood.

Smiling signals to your brain that things are okay, and in return, you start to feel better. It's a physical action that sparks a positive reaction.

Smiling is a sign of a pleasant mood and a positive attitude. When you smile, you naturally feel better, and that shift can move you into a more optimistic mindset. Plus, smiling tells others you're happy—and that energy is contagious. People are drawn to positivity.

So why wait? The time is now. Send out the glow within you—and smile on.

Focus On
The Good

Focus On the Good:

We've all been through terrible times. None of us have had perfect lives. We all go through hard chapters in our lifetime. In every situation, we have a choice: we can let those moments keep us down, or we can rise above them.

The power to shift our perspective lies within our own minds. We can choose to focus on the good in our lives. Sure, things may never be perfect—but there is always something good.

So why not focus more on that instead of dwelling on the negative?

Good is always there. Sometimes, we just have to look a little harder to see it.

So, smile—and focus on the good.

Never Look Back

Never Look Back:

Never look back" is often easier said than done. But what does it really mean? It means exactly what it says.

We all have things in our past that may be painful or negative. But why continue to focus on something that's already behind you or something you can't change? It happened. It's done. And holding onto it only keeps you from moving forward.

Think about it like this: the windshield of a car is much larger than the rearview mirror for a reason. While it's okay to glance back now and then, but your main focus should be on what's ahead—because that's where you're going.

So stop letting the past weigh you down. Let it stay behind you where it belongs. Focus on the positive future that lies in front of you. Smile, focus on the good—and never look back.

Enjoy The Simple Things

Enjoy The Simple Things:

Enjoy the simple things in life. Stop focusing on all the wants. Cars, boats, dream homes—these are all just things. And the truth is, none of us can take any of it with us when we reach the end of our lives.

Dwelling on what you don't have or wish you had won't help you stay positive. Instead, turn your attention to the simple things that truly bring you joy. In the end, those are the things that will matter most.

Simple moments—like spending time in nature, laughing with family, or catching up with friends—create the memories that last a lifetime. These are the things that keep us grounded, grateful, and truly happy.

The simple things are the real treasures. They keep us down to earth—and they help us staying positive.

Say Hello

Say Hello:

Say hello to people—and smile. It's such a simple thing to do, but it can lift your spirits and brighten someone else's day too.

Whether you're in a store, walking through a parking lot, or passing someone on the street, take a moment to acknowledge them with a friendly hello. It's a small gesture, but a powerful one. Kind human interaction has a way of creating connection, spreading positivity, and making the world feel just a little bit warmer.

I've found that I always feel better after a kind exchange like this. And chances are, the other person does too.

So the next time you're out, try it. Say hello to someone. Smile. It might just make both of your days a little better.

Slow Down

Slow Down:

Slow down and take the time to truly take things in. That might sound easy, but it's harder than you think. Life moves fast—we're constantly rushing from one thing to the next. But slowing down is essential to staying positive.

What I mean is: take time to smell the roses. Literally. If you're driving to work and pass a beautiful farm, a peaceful stream, or a scenic view—pause for a moment. Notice it. Appreciate it. Let it lift your mood, even just a little.

We often get so caught up in the hustle of life that we forget to enjoy it. But when you slow down and notice the little things, you reconnect with what matters. It helps boost your morale, improves your outlook, and grounds you in the present.

The rat race can wear you down. Slowing down—even just a little—can help break that cycle. And that small shift can have a big, positive impact on how you feel.

Stop Complaining

Stop Complaining:

Stop complaining about things. Complaining brings you down and solves nothing. The act of complaining only reinforces negative thinking.

Instead of reacting with frustration, pause for a moment and think of a more positive way to handle the situation. This may take some effort, and you might need to really think before you respond—but that moment of reflection can make all the difference.

The more you complain, the less positive you become. If you're faced with a situation that's unpleasant or difficult, do your best to fix it. Stay focused on the solution, look ahead, and smile— knowing you have the power to change the outcome.

Not complaining is probably one of the hardest habits to break, but it's also one of the most powerful ways to stay in a positive state of mind. People who complain often tend to carry a negative outlook. Only you have the power to shift that—for yourself.

Do Not Make Excuses

Do Not Make Excuses:

Don't make excuses for things. Instead of making excuses, admit the problem to yourself and figure out how to fix it. People who constantly make excuses tend to be negative thinkers. Tell yourself, "I can do this," and then get it done. This mindset will help you stay positive.

Making excuses leads to accomplishing nothing.

But if you pause, stay positive about the situation, and work on fixing it, you'll achieve something—and that accomplishment will keep you positive. No one feels good after making excuses. You'll feel better admitting your fault and then taking action to fix it.

Stay Away From Negative People

Stay Away from Negative People:

Negative people have a way of pulling others down. We've all been around someone who constantly complains, criticizes, or sees the worst in every situation. Often, these individuals want you to join them in their negativity—because misery loves company.

It can be especially difficult when these people are close friends or even family members.

You may feel obligated to spend time with them or worry about offending them. But your mental and emotional well-being must come first.

Try to lift them up with a smile or a kind word. Say hello. Show them positivity. But don't allow their energy to drain yours. The truth is, there's only so much you can do for someone who chooses to stay negative. The more time you spend with someone like that, the more likely you are to absorb their energy.

Sometimes, the healthiest thing you can do is walk away. Keep your circle filled with people who inspire, uplift, and support you. When you surround yourself with positive influences, you'll find it easier to stay grounded, motivated, and happy.

We feed off our surroundings—so make sure you're feeding off positivity, not negativity.

Be Happy for Others' Success

Be Happy For Others' Success:

We're all on this journey together. There's no reason to frown upon someone else's success. In fact, when you choose to celebrate others, you invite more positivity into your own life.

Being happy for someone else's achievements doesn't take away from your own. Instead, it creates space for inspiration. Use their success as motivation—not as a reason to feel bitter or envious.

Let it drive you to work harder, to grow, and to believe that good things are possible for you too.

Negativity grows when we compare ourselves in unhealthy ways. But positivity grows when we celebrate others and cheer them on. It's a choice—so why not choose joy over jealousy, and happiness over misery?

Learning to genuinely be happy for others helps you become a more positive person. And that positivity doesn't just benefit you—it lifts up the people around you too.

Be Happy With What You Have

Be Happy with What You Have:

It's easy to focus on what we don't have. But true positivity comes from being grateful for what we do have. Yes, it can be hard sometimes—especially when life feels like it's moving slower than we'd like, or when we see others achieving things we want. But learning to appreciate your life as it is right now can bring lasting peace and happiness.

There will always be someone who seems better off than you.

But remember this: there's also someone out there who wishes they had your life. And when I say "better off," I don't just mean money or possessions. I'm talking about health, relationships, peace of mind, and even the simple things—like having a roof over your head or someone who loves you.

Be happy with life itself. Things can always be worse. The more you focus on what's good, the easier it becomes to stay positive, even during tough times.

Every day you wake up is a gift. No one is promised tomorrow, so be thankful for today.

Get Into
The Sun

Get Into the Sun:

It might sound simple, but getting into the sun can make a big difference in your mood and mindset. It's a natural and powerful way to boost your positivity.

When you spend time in the sunlight, your brain releases a hormone called serotonin—often known as the "feel-good" chemical. Serotonin helps improve your mood and helps you feel calm, focused, and emotionally balanced.

We often underestimate how much a little sunshine can do. Even just a few minutes outside can help break up the stress of a busy day. Let the warmth of the sun wrap around you like a gentle hug from nature. Breathe it in. Feel it on your skin. Smile.

So whenever you get the chance, step outside. Soak up a bit of sunshine. Let it lift your spirit. It's a small habit that can have a big impact on your positivity and well-being. I try and do this everyday.

Be The Best Version Of You

Be The Best Version of You:

Always strive to be the best person you can be. It's easy to fall into the trap of comparing ourselves to others—especially in a world that constantly measures success in likes, numbers, or status. But there will always be someone faster, stronger, or seemingly more successful. That's not the point.

The goal is progress, not comparison.

Focus on being better than you were yesterday.

That's where real growth lives. When you put your energy into becoming the best version of yourself, you stay grounded, motivated, and proud of your journey.

And if there are days when you don't feel your best, it's okay. Use those moments to reflect and adjust. Keep moving forward. As long as you're trying, you're growing.

There's a deep, rewarding feeling that comes from knowing you gave your best.

That feeling helps fuel your positivity and keeps you in a strong, healthy mindset.

So keep showing up. Keep improving. And most importantly—keep being you.

Help
Others

<u>Help Others:</u>

Helping others is one of the most rewarding things you can do. When you see someone in need and choose to help them, it not only benefits them — it lifts you up too. That good feeling you get from lending a hand brings real, lasting positivity into your own life.

And the best part, it's simple. You don't need to wait for someone to ask. If you notice someone struggling, step in. Do it out of kindness. Do it because it's the right thing to do.

Staying positive isn't always about focusing on yourself. Sometimes, the most powerful way to stay positive is by doing good for others. So smile. Show up. Help someone today — not because you have to, but because you want to.

Live Day By Day

Live Day by Day:

Living day by day is exactly what it sounds like — being present, right here and right now. We only get one amazing life, and every day we wake up is a gift, a bonus round we've been blessed with. So don't waste it living in the past. And don't get trapped worrying about a future you can't control.

What you can control is today. Right now.

Stress and regret over what's already happened will only weigh you down. Anxiety about tomorrow will only steal your peace. But choosing to focus on today — and making it count — is one of the best ways to stay in a positive mindset.

Be present. Smile. Be thankful for the day you're in. Win small victories, even if it's just getting out of bed, finishing a task, or encouraging someone else. These moments add up.

Living in the moment isn't just a good idea — it's the most powerful way to stay positive.

Now go out there and live for today.

Self-Care

Self-Care:

Self-care plays a major role in our mental well-being. To stay positive, we must first be happy with ourselves. Self-care can include eating well, exercising, getting enough rest, or learning something new. These actions help boost our mood and bring a sense of accomplishment.

When we look in the mirror and feel the urge to change something—let that be the moment we take action.

The time is now. Don't dwell on the past. Live for today.

The better we feel about ourselves, the more confident we become—and confidence naturally leads to positivity. We must take care of ourselves, because at the end of the day, no one else can do it for us.

This is one of the biggest keys to staying positive in a negative world. So make yourself a priority. Carve out time each day just for you—you deserve it.

Think
Positive

Think Positive:

Think positive—yes, you read that right. Sometimes, you must choose to think positively, even when it feels unnatural. When you approach life with a positive mindset, positive things are more likely to happen. It's not magic— it's perspective.

On the other hand, people who constantly think negatively often struggle to see the good in anything.

Negative thinking breeds negative outcomes. But when you choose to focus on the positive, even in tough situations, your entire outlook begins to shift.

If something doesn't go exactly as planned, try to look for the silver lining. What can you learn from it? How can it make you stronger? Finding the positive side of any situation helps you stay grounded in a better mindset—and that mindset leads to happiness.

The habit of thinking positively, no matter the outcome, has a powerful effect on your mental well-being. So keep this in mind: Think positive—things will get better.

Wave To Strangers

Wave To Strangers:

Waving to strangers really is that simple. It's a small gesture, but it can make a big difference. A wave is a kind, friendly way to acknowledge someone's presence. If you see someone and they see you—just wave. More often than not, they'll wave back. That small connection creates a moment of shared positivity.

Staying positive isn't always just about you.

Spreading kindness to others—especially through small actions—can have a huge impact on your own mood and mindset. When you make someone else feel seen and appreciated, you'll feel better too.

So wave to strangers. Smile. Be kind. It costs nothing, but it means everything.

Be Better Than You Were Yesterday

Be Better Than You Were Yesterday:

Focus on being better than you were yesterday. That's it. You can't control other people—you can only control you. Set small, achievable goals each day that move you forward. Don't worry about what someone else has or what they're doing. Stay focused on your own journey.

Even the smallest improvement, when repeated daily, adds up to something great over time.

We all have room to grow. When you set a goal and accomplish it—even a small one—that's a victory. And those little victories build confidence and fuel a positive mindset.

So take it one step at a time. Keep going. Keep growing. Be better than you were yesterday—you've got this.

Write In A Journal

Write In a Journal:

Take a few minutes each day to write in a journal. It's a simple habit that can have a big impact. Journaling helps you process your thoughts, express your feelings, and reflect on your experiences—especially on those not-so-perfect days.

Staying positive isn't always easy. Sometimes we carry emotions that we don't even realize are weighing us down.

Writing things out helps you release those feelings, clear your mind, and make sense of what you're going through.

Think of your journal as a safe space—just for you. No judgment, no pressure. Just honesty.

So grab a journal, and start writing about your day. The good, the bad, the in-between. You'll be surprised at how much lighter and more focused you feel. At the end of this book, I included journal pages. This way you can try it.

Keep A Good Life Balance

Keep A Good Life Balance:

Maintaining a healthy balance between work, family, and personal time is essential to staying positive. It's not always easy—but it's necessary.

We all have responsibilities. Work, errands, obligations—they're part of life. But so is rest, joy, and connection. Finding a balance between "must-do" tasks and meaningful downtime is what keeps us grounded.

Try not to let these areas blend too much. When you're working, focus on the task at hand. When it's time for family, friends, or just you, be present. Disconnect from the stress and give yourself permission to enjoy those moments. Whether it's laughter with loved ones, or quiet time alone, that separation is vital.

Keeping this balance doesn't just help you stay focused—it helps you stay happy. Life feels better when it's not all work and no play.

So, take time to recharge. Protect your time, protect your joy—and keep your life balanced. You'll thank yourself for it.

<u>Final Thoughts: Staying Positive in a Negative World</u>

Staying positive in a negative world can be easier said than done. At times, it may feel simpler to give in and let the negativity pull us down. But life is short—shorter than we often realize—so why not spend it as positive as we can?

If you're reading this, that means you've made it through 100% of your worst days. Let that sink in.

You've survived the hard times, the heartbreaks, the setbacks— and you're still here. That alone proves your strength.

Does staying positive take work? Absolutely. But the rewards are real. A positive mindset improves your mental well-being, lifts your spirit, and even helps those around you who might be struggling. Positivity is contagious. When we choose to lift others up, we lift ourselves too.

I wrote this little book to help as many people as I can—because sometimes, we all need a pick-me-up. It doesn't take much: a smile, a wave, a simple "hello" can change someone's day—and yours. These small acts pass positivity forward and make the world a little brighter.

Life isn't simple. And your mindset plays a huge role in how you experience each day. Mental health challenges are very real for many people, especially in a world filled with constant negativity. That's why now is the time to make a change—for you.

No one else can do it for you. But you can do it. Start small. Start today. And choose positivity, even in the face of difficulty.

If you're reading this, you woke up today. That alone is something to be thankful for. Don't take life for granted. Get up, be grateful, and face each day with a hopeful heart.

Remember: staying positive doesn't mean pretending everything is perfect. It means choosing hope.

It means taking action. It means building a life filled with people, habits, and tools that support your growth and peace.

Throughout this book, you've learned real, practical ways to shape your mindset, create balance, and find strength in kindness and purpose. Whether you're struggling, growing, or simply trying to get through the day—progress is progress. No step forward is too small.

Still, there may be times when life feels too heavy to carry alone.

And if you ever reach that point, please remember: you are not alone.

If you're struggling, reach out. Call a friend. Talk to someone. And if you don't know where to turn, call or text 988, the Suicide & Crisis Lifeline. Help is available 24/7. There's always someone ready to listen—judgment-free, with compassion and care.

You are not a burden. You are a human being who matters. Your life matters. Your story isn't over yet.

So please, take care of yourself. Stay grounded. Keep growing. And above all—stay positive.

Suicide & Crisis Lifeline

📞 988 (Call or Text)

You Are Not Alone

People Do Care

Thank you for taking the time to read this book. I wrote it with the hope that it could bring a little light to someone's dark day, and a little encouragement to someone who needs it. We all face struggles, but we don't have to face them alone. Always remember you have already beat 100% of your bad days already. Now go out and beat today.

If this book helped you in any way, my mission is complete. Stay positive, stay strong, and never forget—you matter.

With gratitude,

Douglas Supon

Daily Journal

NO MATTER HOW MANY TIMES YOU FALL, YOU CAN STILL RISE

YOU ARE LOVED

THANK YOU

GO Bills

Printed in Dunstable, United Kingdom